W9-API-228

A Guide for Using

Charlotte's Web

in the Classroom

Based on the novel written by E. B. White

*This guide written by **Patsy Carey** and **Susan Kilpatrick***
*Illustrated by **Theresa M. Wright***

Teacher Created Materials, Inc.
6421 Industry Way
Westminster, CA 92683
www.teachercreated.com
©1993 Teacher Created Materials, Inc.
Reprinted, 2001
Made in U.S.A.
ISBN 1-55734-435-3

Table of Contents

Introduction and Sample Lessons

A good book can touch the lives of children like a good friend. The pictures, words, and characters can inspire young minds as they turn to literary treasures for companionship, recreation, comfort, and guidance. Great care has been taken in selecting the books and unit activities that comprise the primary series of *Literature Units*. Teachers who use this literature unit to supplement their own valuable ideas can plan the activities using one of the following methods.

A Sample Lesson Plan

The sample lessons on page 4 provide you with a specific set of lesson plan suggestions. Each of the lessons can take from one to several days to complete and can include all or some of the suggested activities. Refer to the "Suggestions for Using the Unit Activities" on pages 7-12 for information relating to the unit activities.

A Unit Planner

If you wish to tailor the suggestions on pages 7-12 in a format other than that prescribed in the Sample Lesson Plan, a blank unit planner is provided on page 5. On a specific day you may choose the activities you wish to include by writing the activity number or a brief notation about the lesson in the "Unit Activities" section. Space has been provided for reminders, comments, and other pertinent information relating to each day's activities. Reproduce copies of the Unit Planner as needed.

Sample Lesson Plan

Lesson 1

- Introduce the book by using some or all of "Before the Book" unit activities on page 7.
- Read about the author. (page 6)
- Introduce "Blue Ribbon Math" and continue to use throughout the unit. (pages 32-33)
- Discuss the new vocabulary for chapters 1-3. (page 8)

Lesson 2

- Read chapters 1 - 3.
- Write diamante poems about the city and country. (page 26)
- Discuss the story questions for chapters 1 - 3. (page 16)
- Complete "Pamper Your Pet" Fact Chart after reading chapter 2. (page 34)
- Discuss the new vocabulary for chapters 4-6. (page 8)

Lesson 3

- Read chapters 4-6.
- Complete "This Is the Life" Venn diagram (page 38) and write diamante poems (page 26) after reading chapter 4.
- Introduce the song "Some Pig!" (page 42)
- Discuss the story questions for chapters 4-6. (page 16)
- Make "Animal Babies Booklets" after reading chapter 6. (pages 35-36)
- Prepare stick puppets and stick puppet theaters. Use throughout the lessons to retell or review parts of the story. (pages 21-24)
- Discuss the new vocabulary for chapters 7-9. (page 8)

Lesson 4

- Read chapters 7-9.
- Discuss the story questions for chapters 7-9. (page 16)
- Chart students' prior knowledge about spiders and compare this list to new knowledge gained after reading chapters 7-9.
- Introduce and practice pig and spider poems. (page 20)
- Compare insects and arachnids after reading chapter 9. (page 37)
- Create character webs. (page 25)
- Write and display acrostics on "Spin a Yarn" Web. (page 9)

Lesson 5

- Discuss the new vocabulary for chapters 10 - 12. (page 8)
- Read chapters 10 - 12.
- Discuss the story questions for chapters 10 - 12. (page 16)
- Conduct a "Pig Interview." (page 30)
- List constructive ways to solve problems. (page 39)
- Discuss the new vocabulary for chapters 13 - 15. (page 8)
- Introduce Reader's Theater. (pages 43-47)

Lesson 6

- Read chapters 13 - 15.
- Discuss the story questions for chapters 13 - 15. (page 17)
- Practice Reader's Theater. (pages 43-47)
- Discuss the new vocabulary for chapters 16-18. (page 8)
- Begin "3-D Farm Scenes." (page 41)

Lesson 7

- Read chapters 16 - 18.
- Discuss the story questions for chapters 16 -18. (page 17)
- Practice Reader's Theater, song, and poetry. (pages 20, 42-48)
- Discuss the new vocabulary for chapters 19 - 22. (page 8)
- Complete and display "3-D Farm Scenes." (page 41)

Lesson 8

- Read chapters 19 - 22.
- Discuss the story questions for chapters 19 -22. (page 17)
- Use "Story Summary Sentence Strips" to sequence story events. (pages 18-19)
- Learn about story elements with "What's the Story?" (page 31)
- Have students reflect on the characters and events in the story. (page 11, activity 15)
- Prepare recipes for culminating activity. (page 40)
- Present play. See "Suggestions for Presenting Reader's Theater" (page 43) and "After the Book" (page 12).

Unit Planner

Unit Activities

Date:

Notes/Comments

Unit Activities

Date:

Notes/Comments

Unit Activities

Date:

Notes/Comments

Unit Activities

Date:

Notes/Comments

Unit Activities

Date:

Notes/Comments

Unit Activities

Date:

Notes/Comments

Getting to Know...

...the Book

(Charlotte's Web is published in the U.S. by Dell Publishing Company. It is also available in Canada from Doubleday Dell Seal, in UK from Bantam Doubleday Dell, and in Austria lia from Transworld Publishers.)

This heartwarming story of a pig, the little girl who decides to raise him, the devotion of a good friend, and an unlikely assortment of barnyard animals determined to save his life is sure to touch the lives of children and adults.

The Arable's farm is filled with excitement as a new litter of pigs is born. But when Mr. Arable decides to kill the runt of the litter, Fern begs her father to spare his life. She agrees to care for the pig, whom she lovingly names Wilbur. Eventually, Wilbur is moved to Uncle Zuckerman's Farm. Wilbur is sad and lonely, until he is befriended by a clever spider named Charlotte, who promises to save Wilbur's life. Charlotte uses her unique web-spinning talents to write words about Wilbur in her web. People come from miles around to view the amazing words which describe this extraordinary pig. Wilbur wins a prize at the County Fair and his life is spared. Charlotte has one more surprise for Wilbur when they return to the farm—an egg sac filled with hundreds of tiny spider eggs! But Charlotte dies before her children are born, leaving behind her spiderlings, which Wilbur tends until they hatch.

...the Author

E. B. White (Elwyn Brooks White) was born in Mount Vernon, New York, in 1899. After graduating from Cornell University, White travelled around the country and worked as a reporter, writer, and an editor. In 1925, he began writing for *The New Yorker*. Two of his children's books, *Charlotte's Web* (1952) and *The Trumpet of the Swan* (1970), have received many awards and honors. In both books, the animals display human qualities as they talk and act like people. The underlying themes in *Charlotte's Web* and *The Trumpet of the Swan* are love and friendship. E.B. White also wrote *Stuart Little*. He received a special citation from the Pulitzer Prize Committee for his literary contributions.

Suggestions for Using the Unit Activities

Use some or all of the following suggestions to introduce students to *Charlotte's Web* and to extend their appreciation of the book through activities that cross the curriculum. The suggested activities have been divided into three sections to assist the teacher in planning the literature unit.

The sections are:

- **Before the Book:** which includes suggestions for preparing the classroom environment and the students for the literature to be read

- **Into the Book:** which has activities that focus on the book's content, characters, theme, etc.

- **After the Book:** which extends the reader's enjoyment of the book

Before the Book

1. Before you begin the unit, prepare the vocabulary cards, story questions, and sentence strips for the pocket chart activities. (See samples, patterns, and directions on pages 13-19.)

2. Create a spider web wall or bulletin board in the classroom. Directions for making the web and spiders are provided on pages 27-29. Use the web for the "Spin a Yarn" Web activities described on page 9.

3. If you teach thematically, consider using *Charlotte's Web* to explore such themes as "Friendship" and "Feelings."

4. Build background and set the stage by asking the following questions and discussing the students' responses.

   - Who has visited a farm? What did you see? What did you like most about farm life? What did you like least?

   - What is a friend? What do you like about your best friend? Why do you think he or she likes you?

   - Have you ever considered an animal a friend and not just a pet?

5. Display the cover of *Charlotte's Web*. Have the children look for any clues that might convey the story setting.

6. Discuss with the students what they could do if they found a pet that was hurt or weak.

Into the Book

1. Pocket Chart Activities: Story Questions

Develop critical thinking skills with the story questions on pages 16-17. The questions are based on Bloom's Taxonomy and are provided in each of Bloom's Levels of Learning. Reproduce several copies of the pig pattern on page 15 and write a story question on each pig. (See directions on page 14.)

Suggestions for Using the Unit Activities *(cont.)*

Into the Book *(cont.)*

2. Pocket Chart Activities: Vocabulary Cards

Discuss the meaning of the following words in context before reading the chapters in which they are introduced. Make several copies of the blue ribbon pattern on page 15. Write the words below on the ribbons. Display the ribbons on a pocket chart. (See page 13 for directions on making a pocket chart.)

Chapters 1 - 3

runt	injustice	manure	snout	captivity
litter	peered	trough	slops	vanished

Chapters 4 - 6

goslings	inheritance	salutations	decency	hominy
glutton	detested	scheming	lair	compunctions

Chapters 7- 9

loathed	vaguely	oblige	rigid	rambled
sedentary	hysterics	spinnerets	summoning	campaign

Chapters 10 -12

aeronaut	radiant	idiosyncrasy	mercy	scum
miraculous	exertion	bewilderment	descended	bestirred

Chapters 13 -15

secure	alders	thrashing	anxiety	midsection
ascend	rummaging	monotonous	versatile	radial

Chapters 16 -18

blatting	humble	genuine	buttermilk	dragline
aloft	midway	knothole	stowaway	pummeled

Chapters 19 - 22

languishing	gorge	indigestion	meekly	retorted
gigantic	commotion	phenomenon	carousing	triumph

3. Pocket Chart Activities: Story Summary Sentence Strips

Cut out and laminate the sentences on pages 18-19 to use with a pocket chart. Complete some or all of the following activities.
- On the pocket chart, sequence the sentences in the order in which the event happened in the story.
- Use the sentences to retell the story.
- Divide the class into small groups and distribute a few sentence strips to each group. Ask the groups to act out the part of the story to which the sentence refers.

In addition to these activities, you may wish to reproduce the pages and have students read the sentences aloud to a partner or take them home to read to a parent, sibling, etc.

Suggestions for Using the Unit Activities *(cont.)*

4. Stick Puppet Theater/Puppet Patterns

Prepare Stick Puppet Theaters following the suggestions and directions on page 21. Allow the students to construct puppets by coloring and cutting out the puppets and gluing them to tongue depressors. Follow the suggestions for using stick puppets found at the bottom of page 21.

5. Diamante Poetry

Have students create contrast poems by introducing them to the poetic form of the diamante. (The diamante pattern and a poetry sample are provided on page 26.) Model the poetry form and provide practice in using the diamante pattern. Have students write "Country-City" poems after completing the Venn diagram on page 38.

6. "Spin a Yarn" Web Activities

• *At Home Activity*

Templeton scavenged through the trash at the fair in search of new words for Charlotte to spin in her web. Have students search through magazines and newspapers at home for words they can bring to class. These could be words that describe the child or a friend. Encourage students to choose words from a related area of the curriculum, words that begin with a specific letter, parts of speech, etc. Cut out the words. Display them on the "Spin a Yarn" web by gluing each word to a strip of construction paper. Attach the words to spinnerets or to the spider's body on the "Spin a Yarn" Web.

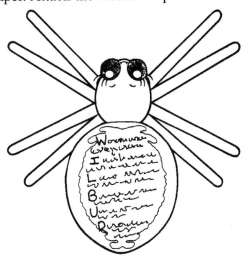

• *Acrostics*

As an alternative to the "At Home Activity," have students create acrostics using the letters from one of the characters' names in Charlotte's Web. Remind them that the phrases they choose should reflect a quality or action of the character.

Completed acrostics can be written in the center of the spider pattern on page 28. (See illustration.) Attach the assembled spiders to the spider web for all to read and enjoy. As an extension, have students create acrostics about themselves and write them on the spiders.

7. "Pig Interview"

Have children conduct a "Pig Interview." (March 1st is National Pig Day.) Allow children to work in pairs to interview a pig; one takes the role of the pig and the other takes the role of the reporter. Encourage the children to be creative and think of unusual and original responses to the questions. Record responses. See questions and student directions on page 30. When interviews are completed, have the teams share the information they have gathered from the interviews with a small group or the entire class. Each child can begin with the statement, "Let me introduce you to_____, the pig."

Suggestions for Using the Unit Activities *(cont.)*

Into the Book *(cont.)*

8. What's the Story?

Have students use the story map on page 31 to determine the setting, characters, problem, and solution elements in *Charlotte's Web*. If students are not familiar with this format, model the process with them using the example on this page or one of your own choosing.

1. Setting: The Arables' Farm, The Zuckermans' Farm, The state Fair

2. Characters: Wilbur, Charlotte, Templeton, Fern, Lurvy, Henry, Avery, The Arables, The Zuckermans, the barnyard animals

3. Problem: Wilbur learns he is being fattened up because he is to be killed by his owner, Mr. Zuckerman. He doesn't know how to save himself and he is very worried.

4. Solution: Wilbur meets Charlotte, a beautiful spider. She spins words in her web and everyone thinks Wilbur is "some pig." He wins a prize at the fair and his life is saved.

9. Blue Ribbon Math Game

Use the pig pattern on page 32 to make a class set of Blue Ribbon Math gameboards. Reproduce and cut out the pattern on pink construction or index paper. Write math fact answers on the blue ribbons. (Note: No two gameboard cards should be identical.) Laminate the gameboards for durability.

Reproduce and cut out the prize ribbon cards on page 33 and write a math fact on each. Distribute a gameboard to each student. Provide students with "markers" such as dried beans, plastic discs, paper squares, etc. Follow the instructions on page 33 for playing the Blue Ribbon Math game.

10. "Pamper Your Pet" Fact Chart

Ask your class to brainstorm the ways Fern took care of Wilbur. List student ideas on the board. Have some of the students name their pets. As a whole-class or cooperative group activity, allow students to brainstorm food, habitat, exercise, and other ways to care for their pets. You may wish to model the activity first by choosing a pet and noting on a chart or chalkboard items to consider while caring for a pet. Have students record the information on the Fact Chart on page 34.

11. Animal Babies Booklet

Check for understanding by matching adult animals and their babies. Reproduce and distribute one copy of page 35 and three copies of page 36 to each student. To assemble the booklets, have students follow the directions on page 35. When booklets are completed, ask students to read them to a partner and/or take them home to read.

Suggestions for Using the Unit Activities *(cont.)*

Into the Book *(cont.)*

12. Arthropods: Insect/Arachnid Comparison

Discuss with the class the following terms: arachnid, insect, arthropod, spinneret, compound eye, antennae. Provide reference materials and pictures of insects and arachnids. Have students work in small groups or pairs to locate information that will help them complete "A Look at Arthropods" (page 37). Ask groups to share their answers and other facts they may have gathered.

13. "This Is the Life!" Venn Diagram

Have students complete the Venn diagram on page 38 by writing in the appropriate areas how the two characters are alike and how they are different. This activity may be presented to the whole class, or you may wish to have the class work in small groups and share their ideas when they are done.

14. Problem Solving

Discuss constructive ways in which students can solve their problems. Reproduce page 39 and ask students to list in the box helpful suggestions for solving their problems. (See sample responses on the right.) Have students share their ideas with each other.

Ways I can Solve My Problems!
1. I can walk away from an argument.
2. I can talk it over with someone.
3. I can say "I'm sorry".
4. I can ask a grownup for help.
5. I can try doing something else.
6. I can suggest a compromise.
7. I can listen to the other person.
8. I can wait for a solution.
9. I can use humor.
10. I can "draw straws" or "flip a coin." (use chance)

15. Blue Ribbon Writing

After reading *Charlotte's Web,* have students reflect on the characters and events of the story, and about the meaning of friendship. Make a blue ribbon stencil pattern a little larger than the size of notebook paper. Trace and cut out the pattern on pieces of blue construction paper. Have students write their thoughts about one of the following statements (or choose one of your own).

Attach completed writings to the centers of the blue ribbons. Display the ribbons on a wall or assemble them into a "Blue Ribbon Writing Class Book."

- I would rather be Charlotte than Wilbur.
- I would rather be Wilbur than Charlotte.
- My favorite character was_____
- Charlotte was a good friend to Wilbur.
- I am a good friend because I...
- When I go to a county fair I...
- A good friend always...

Suggestions for Using the Unit Activities *(cont.)*

After the Book

Culminating Activities

Celebrate the literature unit with a day of enjoyment for students, teachers, and parents. Have students present the Reader's Theater production of *Charlotte's Web*, complete with a play, poetry, music, and food. Send student-made invitations to other classes, teachers, and parents. Include the following preparations and activities.

1. Recite Poetry

Reproduce the poems "Pig Extraordinaire" and "Spider Extraodinaire" (page 20). Divide the class into two groups. Have one group choral read "Pig Extraordinaire" to the other group. Then have the second group read "Spider Extraordinaire" to the first group. Discuss the meaning and contents of both poems. As part of the culminating activities, assign a student, a small group, or half the class to recite each of the poems at the close of the Reader's Theater production. For additional poems on friends and friendship refer to "How Many, How Much," and "Friendship" in Shel Silverstein's *A Light in the Attic* (Harper and Row, 1981).

2. Learn a New Song

Reproduce the song "Some Pig!" on page 42. Practice the music and lyrics with the class. Have the class sing "Some Pig!" following the Reader's Theater script.

3. First Prize Recipes

Prepare recipes for "Pigs-in-a-Blanket," "Quick-and-Easy Fruit Shake," and "Buttermilk Pancakes." Serve these First Prize Recipes following the Reader's Theater production.

4. 3-D Farm Scenes

Using the materials and directions on page 41, have students make farm scenes and animals that can be displayed for visiting parents and classes to see.

5. Reader's Theater Script

Use the Reader's Theater script on pages 44-47 to involve the students in drama. Suggestions for implementing a reader's theater format and script are provided on page 43. Use the follow-up questions below to discuss the qualities of a good friend.

- What makes a good friend?
- Are you a good friend? Tell why.
- Should you do something just because another person can do something for you? (Refer to Templeton's motivations for helping the other animals.)
- How did Charlotte solve Wilbur's problem? What are some ways you can solve your own problems?

Pocket Chart Activities

Prepare a pocket chart for storing and using the vocabulary cards, the story question cards, and the sentence strips.

How to Make a Pocket Chart

If a commercial pocket chart is unavailable, you can make a pocket chart if you have access to a laminator. Begin by laminating a 24" x 36" (60 cm x 90 cm) piece of colored tagboard. Run about 20" (50 cm) of additional plastic. To make nine pockets, cut the clear plastic into nine equal strips. Space the strips equally down the 36" (90 cm) length of the tagboard. Attach each strip with cellophane tape along the bottom and sides. This will hold sentence strips, word cards, etc., and can be displayed in a learning center or mounted on a chalk tray for use with a group. When your pocket chart is ready, use it to display the sentence strips, vocabulary words, and question cards. A sample chart is provided below.

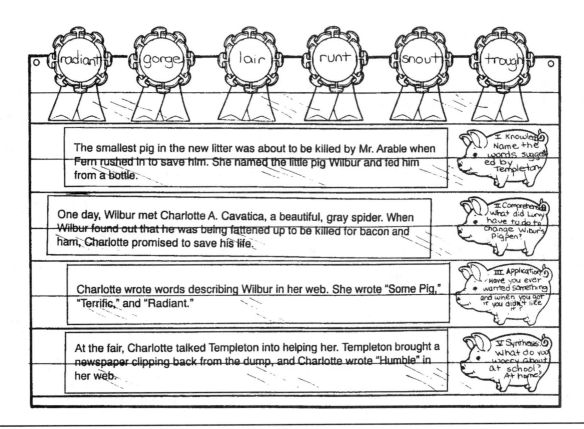

How to Use the Pocket Chart

---

1. On blue construction or index paper, reproduce the ribbon-shaped pattern on page 15. Make vocabulary cards as directed on page 8. (You may wish to include the chapter in which the word appears.) To familiarize the children with difficult words and their meanings, present the vocabulary cards for each chapter before reading the corresponding chapters. Help students understand the word meanings by providing context clues.

The blue ribbon pattern can be used to make "Amazing Author," "Wonderful Worker," "Great Reader," and other appropriate awards or incentives.

Pocket Chart Activities *(cont.)*

2. Reproduce several copies of the pig pattern (page 15) on six different colors of construction paper. Use a different paper color to represent each of Bloom's Levels of Learning.

For example:

I.   Knowledge *(green)*

II. Comprehension *(pink)*

III. Application *(lavender)*

IV. Analysis *(orange)*

V.   Synthesis *(blue)*

VI. Evaluation *(yellow)*

Write a chapter question from pages 16 or 17 on the appropriate color-coded pig. Write the level of the question, the question, and the chapter section on the body of the pig, as shown in the example above.

Use the pig-shaped cards after the corresponding chapters have been read to provide opportunities for the children to develop and practice higher level critical thinking skills. The cards can be used with some or all of the following activities.

• Use a specific color-coded set of cards to question students at a particular Level of Learning.

• Have a child choose a card, read it aloud, or give it to the teacher to read aloud. The child answers the question or calls on a volunteer to answer it.

• Pair children. The teacher reads a question. Children take turns with their partners responding to the question.

• Play a game. Divide the class into teams. Ask for a response to a question written on one of the question cards. Teams score a point for each appropriate response. If question cards have been prepared for several different stories, mix up the cards and ask team members to respond by naming the story that relates to the question. Extra points can be awarded if a team member answers the question as well.

3. Use the sentence strips to practice oral reading and sequencing of the story events. Reproduce pages 18-19. If possible, laminate the sentence strips for durability. Cut out the sentence strips or prepare sentences of your own to use with the pocket chart.

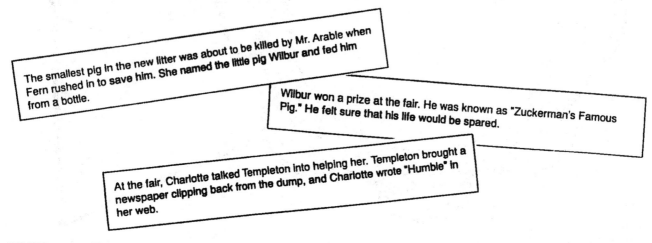

Pocket Chart Patterns

See pages 7 and 8 for directions.

Story Questions

Use the following questions with the suggested activities on page 14. Prepare the pig pattern (page 15) and write a different question from the appropriate chapters on each of the pigs.

Chapters 1-3

I.	*Knowledge:*	How did Fern treat Wilbur like a baby?
II.	*Comprehension:*	What does "do away with" mean?
III.	*Application:*	Have you ever wanted something and when you got it, you didn't like it? Explain.
IV.	*Analysis:*	Identify the results of the bad things that the goose encouraged Wilbur to do.
V.	*Synthesis:*	Tell why Wilbur was not happy with his freedom.
VI.	*Evaluation:*	What are the advantages of having a pet like Wilbur? What are the disadvantages?

Chapters 4-6

I.	*Knowledge:*	How did Wilbur find his mysterious friend?
II.	*Comprehension:*	Describe how Templeton spends his time.
III.	*Application:*	Have you ever felt like you needed a friend? What did you do about it? Explain.
IV.	*Analysis:*	Would you rather share a meal with Charlotte or Wilbur? Tell why.
V.	*Synthesis:*	Tell the good and bad qualities Wilbur discovered in Charlotte.
VI.	*Evaluation:*	Would you trust Templeton? Why or why not?

Chapters 7-9

I.	*Knowledge:*	Who was going to save Wilbur?
II.	*Comprehension:*	Why is Wilbur unable to spin a web?
III.	*Application:*	Why didn't Mr. Arable worry about Fern? Do fathers worry about things that worry mothers?
IV.	*Analysis:*	What would your mother do if you told her about talking animals? Do you believe that animals talk to each other? To people? How do they communicate?
V.	*Synthesis:*	Tell what you would do to save Wilbur's life.
VI.	*Evaluation:*	How did you feel when the sheep said that Wilbur was going to be killed?

Chapters 10-12

I.	*Knowledge:*	What words did Charlotte write in her web?
II.	*Comprehension:*	Explain what caused the explosion in the barn?
III.	*Application:*	How did the miracle spider web change life for Wilbur and the Zuckermans?
IV.	*Analysis:*	What happened when people found out about the words in the web?
V.	*Synthesis:*	How does Charlotte propose to save Wilbur's life? What could you plan to do?
VI.	*Evaluation:*	Why does Templeton agree to save Wilbur's life?

Story Questions *(cont.)*

Chapters 13 -15

I.   *Knowledge:* Name the words suggested by Templeton.

II. *Comprehension:* What did Lurvy have to do to change Wilbur's pigpen?

III. *Application:* Identify what Wilbur and Charlotte were worried about in the "crickets" chapter.

IV. *Analysis:* Why did Charlotte feel that she should not go to the fair with Wilbur? What was wrong with the descriptive words suggested by Templeton (crunchy preshrunk, radiant)?

V.   *Synthesis:* What do you worry about at school? At home?

VI. *Evaluation:* Fern said that her best friends were in the barn. What qualities do you look for in a best friend?

Chapters 16-18

I.   *Knowledge:* What are some of the clues that the author uses to let the reader know that Charlotte is not herself?

II. *Comprehension:* Why did Charlotte and Templeton decide to go to the fair?

III. *Application:* Why did Fern have the best time ever at the fair? What do you think you would like best at a fair?

IV. *Analysis:* Explain why Wilbur fainted in the story.

V.   *Synthesis:* What words do you think best describe Wilbur?

VI. *Evaluation:* How has Fern changed since the beginning of the story?

Chapters 19-22

I.   *Knowledge:* What are some of the ways that Templeton was helpful in the story?

II. *Comprehension:* What were Charlotte's two jobs at the fair?

III. *Application:* How have you won/earned a special prize, trophy, or award?

IV. *Analysis:* Why did Wilbur get Templeton to take down Charlotte's egg sac? Describe the problems facing each of the main characters: Fern, Wilbur, Charlotte, and Templeton.

V.   *Synthesis:* What is the most important thing to remember about the story? If you could, how would you change the ending of this story?

VI. *Evaluation:* How did you feel when Charlotte died? What did Charlotte teach Wilbur?

Story Summary Sentence Strips

See page 8 (activity 3) for directions.

The smallest pig in the new litter was about to be killed by Mr. Arable when Fern rushed in to save him. She named the little pig Wilbur and fed him from a bottle.	One day, Wilbur met Charlotte A. Cavatica, a beautiful, gray spider. When Wilbur found out that he was being fattened up to be killed for bacon and ham, Charlotte promised to save his life.	Charlotte wrote words describing Wilbur in her web. She wrote "Some Pig," "Terrific," and "Radiant."	At the fair, Charlotte talked Templeton into helping her. Templeton brought a newspaper clipping back from the dump, and Charlotte wrote "Humble" in her web.

Story Summary Sentence Strips *(cont.)*

See page 8 (activity 3) for directions.

Wilbur won a prize at the fair. He was known as "Zuckerman's Famous Pig." He felt sure that his life would be spared.

Charlotte was nearing the end of her life. She knew she would soon die. Wilbur asked Templeton to help him get the egg sac so they could take it back to the farm.

Charlotte had been a loyal friend to the very end. Wilbur knew that he would never forget her.

One spring morning, Charlotte's babies were born. Most of them floated away on tiny silk balloons. Joy, Aranea, and Nellie chose to stay with Wilbur and live in the barn cellar.

"Best Friend" Poems

Pig Extraordinaire
Wilbur, you are "radiant,"
"Some pig" is what you are.
Absolutely wonderful,
You're certainly a star.
Wilbur, you're "terrific!"
You deserve top prize.
Your talent is exceptional,
You are a perfect size.
Wilbur, you are "humble,"
A pig beyond compare,
Innocent and charming,
A pig extraordinaire.
                    –By Susan Kilpatrick

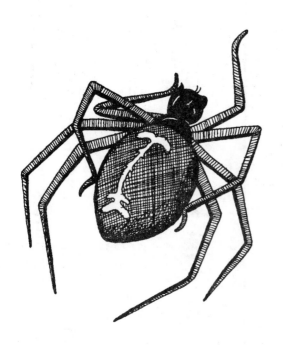

Spider Extraordinaire
Charlotte, you're amazing,
You know just what to say.
You're skillful and intelligent,
You truly saved the day!
Charlotte, you're miraculous,
Simply one of a kind.
A more ideal companion,
A pig could never find.
Charlotte, you're incredible,
A friend beyond compare.
You're talented and clever,
A spider extraodinaire.
                    –By Susan Kilpatrick

Stick Puppet Theaters

Make a class set of puppet theaters (one for each child), or make one theater for every 2-4 children.

Materials: 22" x 28" (56 cm x 71 cm) pieces of colored poster board (enough for each student or group of students); markers, crayons, or paints; scissors or craft knife

Directions:

1. Fold the poster board about 8" (20 cm) in from each of the shorter sides.

2. Cut a "window" in the center of the theater, large enough to accommodate two or three puppets. (See illustration.)

3. Let the children personalize and decorate their own theaters.

4. Laminate the theaters to make them more durable. You may wish to send the theaters home at the end of the year or save them to use year after year.

Suggestions for Using the Puppets and Puppet Theaters:

- Prepare the stick puppets using the directions on page 22. Use the puppets and the puppet theaters with the Reader's Theater script on pages 44-47. (Let small groups of children take turns reading the parts and using the stick puppets.)

- Let children experiment with the puppets by telling the story in their own words.

- Read quotations from the book or make statements about the characters and ask students to hold up the stick puppets represented by the quotes or statements.

Stick Puppet Patterns

Directions: Reproduce the patterns on index paper or construction paper. Color the patterns. Cut along the dotted lines. To complete the stick puppets, glue each pattern to a tongue depressor or craft stick. Use stick puppets with puppet theaters and/or the Reader's Theater script.

Stick Puppet Patterns *(cont.)*

See page 22 for directions.

Stick Puppet Patterns *(cont.)*

See page 22 for directions.

Name_____

Character Web

Directions: Choose a character from *Charlotte's Web*. Write his or her name in the center of the web. With a partner, brainstorm ideas about what the character is like—what he or she does, the way the character acts, etc. Write a different idea in each section of the web. Share your character web with the class.

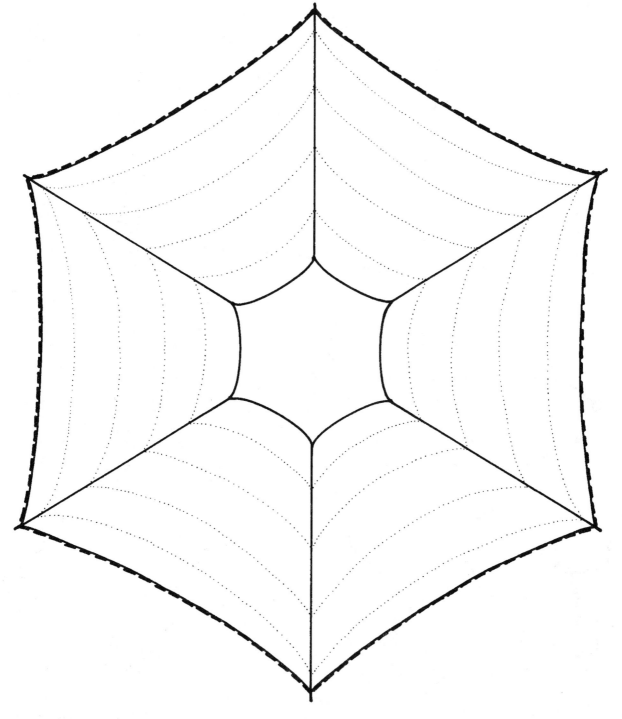

Diamante Poetry

The diamante (dee-ah-mahn-tay) pattern is a seven line contrast poem having a diamond shape. The pattern structure is as follows:

1st line: one noun for which you know a contrasting noun

2nd line: two adjectives which describe the subject

3rd line: three participles (-ing or -ed words) which describe the subject

4th line: two nouns related to the subject and two nouns related to the opposite of the subject (see below)

5th line: three more participles (-ing or -ed words) which describe line four

6th line: two adjectives which describe the contrasting noun (the last word in line seven)

7th line: the final noun that is in contrast to the subject

Sample Diamante:

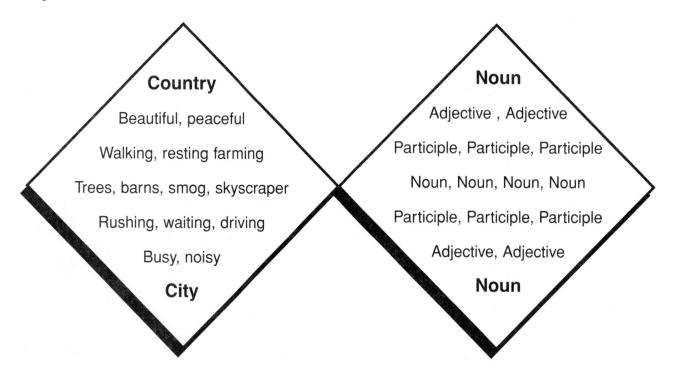

Extension: After students have written diamante poetry contrasting country and city life, have them try to create poetry using one or more of the following contrasting subjects:

day—night	fire—ice	play—work
mom—dad	land—water	earth—space
mountains—plains	forest—desert	sadness—happiness

"Spin a Yarn" Web

Create a classroom spider web following the directions below. Reproduce pages 28 and 29. Have students cut out and assemble spiders. Use with activities described on page 9.

Directions:

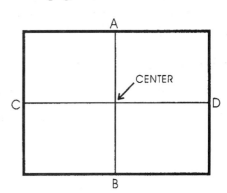

1. Cover a large bulletin board or wall area with a light-colored background.

2. Mark the center points of each side of the bulletin board or wall space and attach a piece of colored yarn from the center point of one side to the center point of the opposite side (A to B, C to D) as shown. Staple the yarn at the ends, making sure that the yarn is pulled fairly tightly.

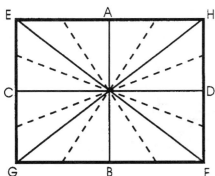

3. Begin to criss-cross the yarn. First connect E to F; then G to H. Continue making the web until you have a total of about 16 evenly-spaced spokes radiating from the center.

4. To create a finished appearance, add a border to the bulletin board.

5. Starting from the center and moving in a clockwise direction, weave the rest of the web in a spiral pattern. Alternate under and over each consecutive spoke. Do not pull too tightly. When you reach the border, or when you feel that you have enough web, cut and tie off the yarn.

6. Place a small drop of glue wherever the spirals of yarn touch the spokes to secure the shape of the web.

7. Have the students construct spiders using the patterns on pages 28 and 29. Staple the spider feet to the web. Additional spiders can be hung around and in front of the web.

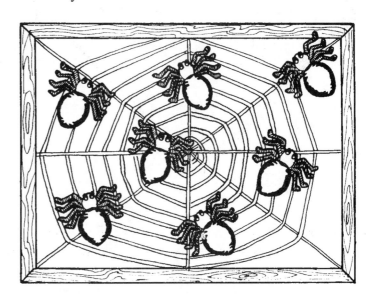

Spider Pattern

Directions for Spider's Body:

Use a black crayon to color the area of the spider's body outside the design. Cut out the spider's body.

Directions for Spider's Legs:

Reproduce the pattern on page 29. Use a crayon to color the spider's legs black. Cut out the pattern. Fold each leg down along the dotted line at the "knee." Fold each leg up along the dotted lines at the "foot." Glue the spider's body over its legs as indicated.

Spider Pattern *(cont.)*

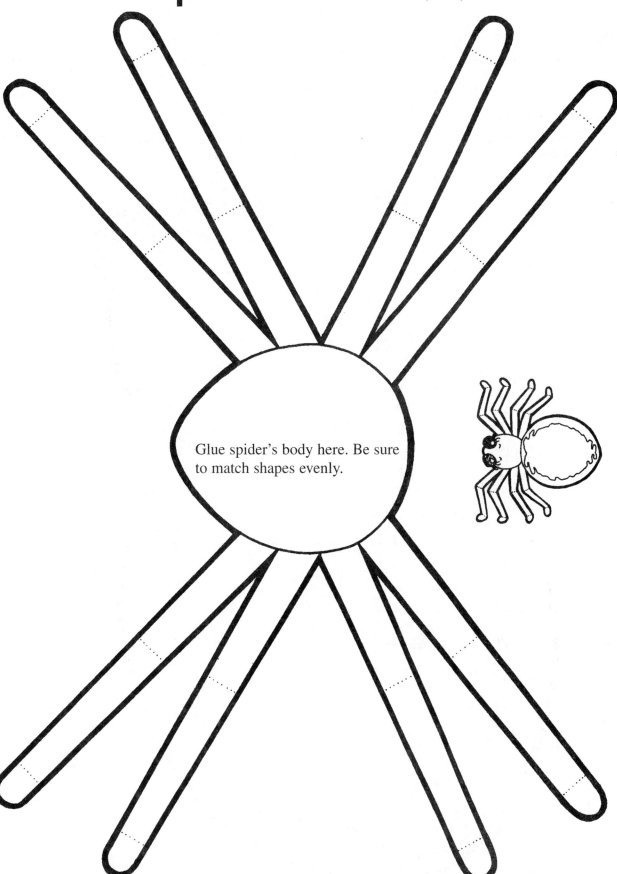

Glue spider's body here. Be sure to match shapes evenly.

"Pig Interview"

Directions: For this activity you will work with a partner. One of you will take the role of a pig while the other takes the role of a reporter. The reporter asks the questions below and records the pig's answers. When you are finished, reverse the roles of the pig and the reporter. Record your answers in the correct boxes (Reporter #1 or Reporter #2) to the right of the questions.

Questions	Reporter #1 _____ (name)	Reporter #2 _____ (name)
What is your name?		
Where do you live?		
What are your favorite foods?		
What do you like to do with your family? With your friends?		
Who are your friends?		
Where do you like to go on vacation?		
What books do you like to read?		
How do you like to spend your time?		
What do you like about yourself?		
What would you like to change about yourself?		

Name_____

What's the Story?

Blue Ribbon Math

Follow the directions on page 10 to prepare the gameboard on this page.

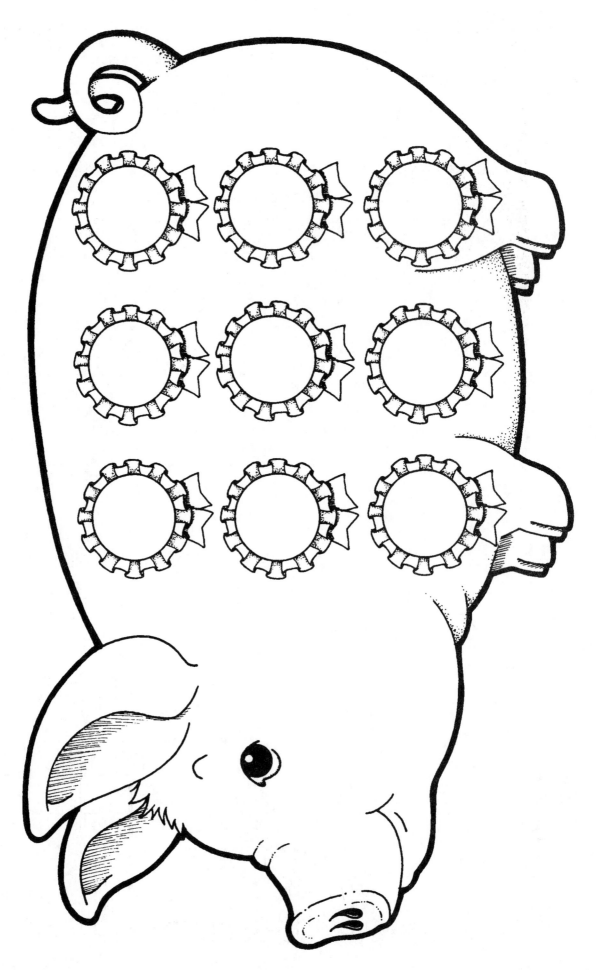

Blue Ribbon Math (cont.)

Follow the directions on page 10 to prepare the prize-ribbon cards on this page. Reproduce as many cards as necessary to play the game.

How to Play the Blue Ribbon Math Game

Distribute a gameboard to each student. Place all prize ribbon cards face down on a playing surface. Choose a student to be the "caller." As a fact is called, the students cover the corresponding answer ribbon on the gameboard with a "marker." Game continues until a player marks three ribbons in a row—horizontally, vertically, or diagonally—and calls a name chosen by the teacher or the class.

Teacher: Use after Chapter 2. See page 10 for directions.

Name_____

"Pamper Your Pet" Fact Chart

Animal	Food	Habitat	Exercise	Other Ways To Care for the Animal

Animal Babies Booklets

Directions:

1. Match the adult animals and their babies by numbering the boxes. (See example.)

2. Cut out the boxes and glue them into the "Animal Babies Booklet" on page 36. Be sure to place the matching adult and baby on the same page.

3. Write the animal names on the booklet pages. Draw pictures of the animals.

4. Cut the pages along the dashed lines. You should have 6 booklet pages.

5. Make a cover by folding a piece of construction paper in half from top to bottom. Decorate the cover and title it "My Animal Babies Booklet." Staple the booklet pages inside the cover.

6. Read your "Animal Babies Booklet" to a partner.

Geese `1`	**piglets**
Pigs	**lambs**
Horses	**goslings** `1`
Sheep	**polliwogs**
Cows	**foals**
Frogs	**calves**

Animal Babies Booklet *(cont.)*

Glue adult
animal name
here.

Glue baby
animal name
here.

_____
(adult animal name)

have

_____
baby animal name

Illustration

Glue adult
animal name
here.

Glue baby
animal name
here.

_____
(adult animal name)

have

_____
baby animal name

Illustration

Name_____

A Look at Arthropods

Directions: Locate information about arachnids and insects that will help you complete this page. Share your findings with the class.

Insect	**Arachnid**

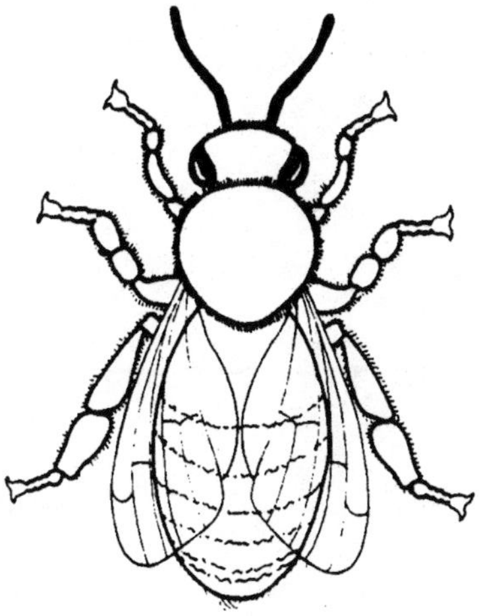

____ number of body parts   ____ number of body parts

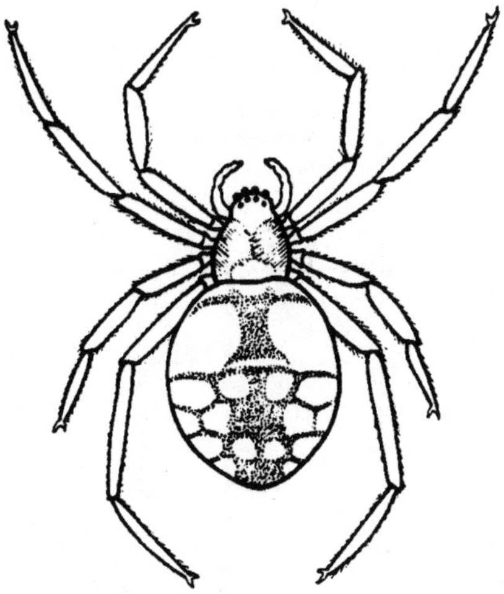

____ number of legs   ____ number of legs

____ number of eyes   ____ number of eyes

____ **yes no** usually has wings   ____ **yes no** usually has wings
        (circle one)   (circle one)

____ **yes no** usually has spinnerets   ____ **yes no** usually has spinnerets
        (circle one)   (circle one)

On the lines below, compare insects and arachnids. Use the following sentence to begin writing about how insects differ.

Insects are different from arachnids in several ways._____

_____

_____

_____

_____

Teacher: Use after Chapter 4. Have students use the information from this page to write diamante poetry. (See sample on page 26.)

Name _____

This Is the Life!

Directions:

Think about ways in which city life and country life are the same and ways in which they are different. Write your ideas in the correct sections of the pictures below.

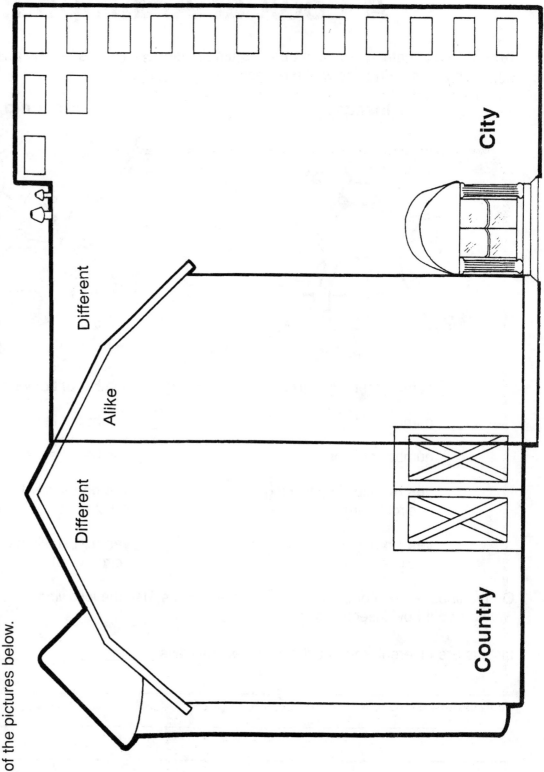

City

Different

Alike

Different

Country

38

Name_____

What's the Problem?

Directions: Charlotte worked hard to solve the problem of how to save Wilbur's life. Think of some ways you can solve problems. Work by yourself, with a partner, or with a group. Write your ideas in the box below. If you need more space, use the back of your paper. Be ready to share and discuss your ideas with the class.

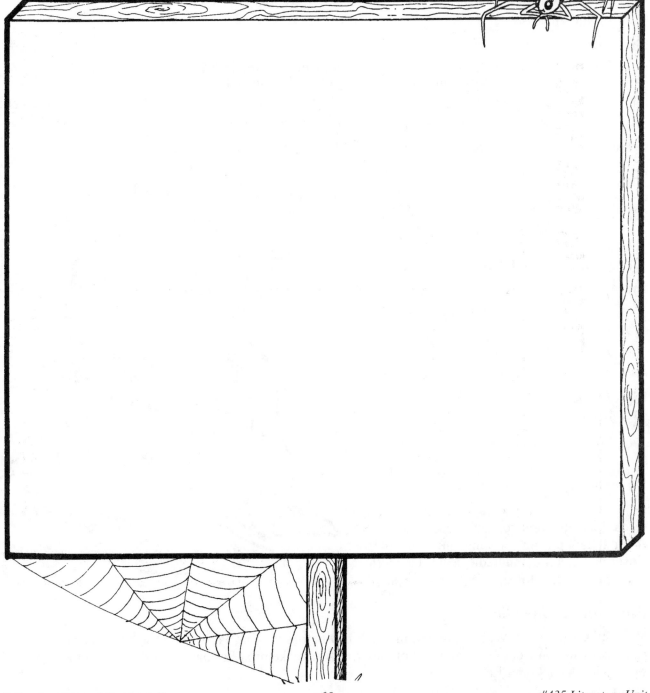

First Prize Recipes

Perhaps Fern's mother could have won a first-place blue ribbon at the county fair with these recipes.

Pigs-in-a-Blanket

Ingredients:

- cocktail hot dogs (enough for each student to have one or two)
- 4 packages of refrigerated crescent-shaped rolls

Equipment:

- small cookie sheets
- toaster oven (If a standard oven is available, a large cookie sheet can be used.)
- plastic knives

Directions:

- Remove rolls from package. If necessary, cut them into smaller triangles proportionate to the size of the hot dogs. Place one miniature hot dog on each flattened crescent roll triangle.
- Roll dough around hot dog. Bake according to directions on package until dough is golden brown.
- Optional: Provide mustard and catsup for added taste.

Serve your "Pigs-in-a Blanket" with one of the following beverages.

Pink Lemonade

Prepare pink lemonade as directed on container.

Serve in paper or plastic cups.

Quick-and-Easy Fruit Shake

Ingredients:

- 2 cups (500 mL) vanilla ice cream
- 1 orange
- 1 (16 oz./450 g) can fruit cocktail
- 2 cups (500 mL) pineapple-orange juice

Equipment:

- bowl
- blender
- mixing spoon

Directions:

Before using the orange, remove the peel and any seeds. Place the orange, vanilla ice cream, fruit cocktail, and pineapple-orange juice in a blender. Cover and blend the ingredients until smooth. Pour the shakes into paper or plastic cups.

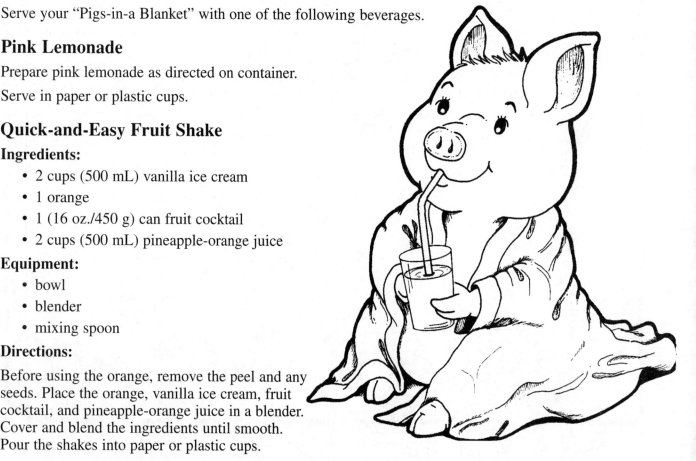

Buttermilk Pancakes

Mrs. Zuckerman gave Wilbur a buttermilk bath just before the fair. Prepare and serve buttermilk pancakes using any commercial brand of buttermilk pancake mix. Follow directions on package and serve with "Quick-and-Easy Fruit Shake."

3-D Farm Scenes

Let children work individually, in pairs, or in small groups to construct 3-sided country scenes. (See sample below.) Students can use cardboard or poster board folded in thirds and designed to create a country-farm background.

Make and decorate play dough animals (pigs, spiders, geese, rats, etc.) and people to place in the foreground. Prepare the play dough recipe on this page or use a commercial brand. Display the "3-D Farm Scenes" around the room.

Super, Fantastic, Never-Fail, Practically-Perfect Play Dough

Materials:

- 3 cups (700 mL) flour
- 1½ cups (350 mL) salt
- 2 tablespoons (30 mL) cream of tartar
- 2 tablespoons (30 mL) oil
- 3 cups (700 mL) water
- desired food coloring
- saucepan
- heat source
- wooden spoon
- covered containers

Directions:

Combine flour, salt, and cream of tartar in large mixing bowl. Mix oil, water, and food coloring together and add to dry ingredients in bowl. Mix thoroughly. Stir the mixture constantly over medium heat, using a wooden spoon. When the dough begins to stick together enough to form a ball, remove it from the heat source but continue stirring. Place the ball of dough on a floured surface. Knead the dough as it cools. The dough will be soft and pliable for molding into whatever shapes are needed for a project.

You can make the dough in advance of an activity and store it in the refrigerator. It also keeps well in a covered container in the freezer. Use the dough recipe for projects throughout the year.

"Some Pig!"

©1992 Mary Ellen Hicks *(used by permission)*

Verse 2:   If you believe you're radiant,
Then let your bright line shine.
So don't feel down,
No need to frown.
Remember you're no swine!

Verse 3:   Now you can still be humble,
Whether rich or poor.
Just be a friend,
Right to the end.
Remember you're no boar!

Suggestions for Presenting Reader's Theater

Reader's Theater is an exciting and easy method of providing students with the opportunity to perform a play while minimizing the use of props, sets, costumes, or memorization. Students read the dialogue of the characters, narrator, chorus, etc., from a book or prepared script. The dialogue may be read verbatim from the book just as the author has written it, or an elaboration may be written by the performing students. Sound effects and dramatic voices can make these much like radio plays.

In a Reader's Theater production, everyone in the class can be involved in some way. The eleven speaking parts, poems on page 20, and the song on page 42 maximize student involvement. Encourage class members to participate in "off-stage" activities, such as greeting the audience and assisting behind the-scenes. Although costumes are not necessary in a reader's theater production, your students may wish to wear simple "costume props." Here are some suggestions:

Charlotte—black leotard

Wilbur—pig nose, paper-plate mask, ears

Templeton—rat ears

Old Sheep—lamb ears or wooly-looking jacket

Lurvy and Mr. Zuckerman—overalls

Fern—overalls or simple dress

The children can wear signs around their necks indicating their speaking parts. Prepare signs by writing the reader's character on a piece of construction paper. Staple a necklace-length piece of yarn to the top of the paper.

If you are presenting the program to another class or to parents, the group of singers can stand off to one side. If you are presenting the play in your own classroom, the audience and the readers join together in singing the song.

You may wish to pre-record the song that will be sung following the play. It will be necessary to have the tape recorder ready; test the tape and recorder prior to the performance. Keep in mind that students may need copies of the music and lyrics if you plan on a live performance.

Reader's Theater Script for Charlotte's Web

Cast of Characters:

Announcer	Fern	Lurvy
Narrator 1	Old Sheep	Mr. Zuckerman
Narrator 2	Wilbur	Templeton
Narrator 3	Charlotte	

Announcer: Welcome to our Reader's Theater presentation of *Charlotte's Web* by E. B. White. Our readers are as follows: *(Announcer lists the cast of readers. Children walk "on stage" as they are introduced and stand in the correct order.)*

Narrator 1: *Charlotte's Web* is the story of a shy, modest pig named Wilbur and a beautiful gray spider named Charlotte.

Narrator 2: Wilbur and Charlotte both lived on a farm with several other animals—a goose, a gander, some goslings, an old sheep, some lambs, and a rat named Templeton.

Narrator 3: Fern, the farmer's daughter, often came to the barnyard and sat on a stool watching and listening to the animals. She especially loved Wilbur.

Fern: You're looking fine and plump today, Wilbur. Your food must be agreeing with you.

Old Sheep: Don't you know what they're fattening you up for Wilbur?

Wilbur: No. What are you talking about?

Old Sheep: They're going to turn you into bacon and ham! Everyone is in on it—including John Arable.

Wilbur: *(sobbing):* Fern's father? Oh, no! I can't believe it! Why would ANYONE want to kill me?

Fern: Oh, Wilbur, I can't believe it either. I'll talk to my father. Don't cry!

Old Sheep: It's true, Wilbur. They're planning to kill you at Christmastime.

Wilbur: Stop! I don't want to die! Save me, somebody! Help me!

Charlotte: Oh quiet down, Wilbur.

Wilbur: *(screaming):* How can I be quiet! Is it true, Charlotte? Are they planning to kill me at Christmastime?

Charlotte: Well, the old sheep usually knows what she is talking about.

Wilbur: I don't want to die, Charlotte! I LOVE my manure pile! I LOVE my friends! I LOVE the fragrant air and the warmth of the sun!

Old Sheep: You LOVE to make a lot of noise, too!

Reader's Theater Script for Charlotte's Web *(cont.)*

Fern:	Oh, poor Wilbur. We all love you so much. Please don't cry.
Wilbur:	*(screaming):* I'm too young to die!
Charlotte:	You shall NOT die, Wilbur.
Wilbur:	What? Who's going to save me?
Charlotte:	I am.
Wilbur:	How? Tell me how.
Fern:	Oh, yes. We all want to know how. Tell us, please.
Charlotte:	I'm not sure just yet, but I want you to quiet down and stop carrying on in such a childish way. I can't stand hysterics.
Narrator 1:	Charlotte thought and thought, day after day. She sat by the hour waiting for an idea to come to her.
Narrator 2:	She had promised Wilbur she would save his life, and she was determined to keep her promise to him.
Narrator 3:	Charlotte was, by nature, very patient. She knew from experience that if she waited long enough a fly would come into her web. Charlotte was sure that if she was patient once again, an idea would come her way. And sure enough, one morning in the middle of July, it did.
Charlotte:	I know how to save Wilbur's life. I'll play a trick on Zuckerman. If I can trick a bug, I can trick a person. After all, humans are not as smart as bugs.
Wilbur:	I wonder what Charlotte means. She is so clever, but I don't understand.
Narrator 1:	That night while everyone slept, Charlotte worked on her web. She tore a large section out and wove the silken threads into something new and amazing.
Narrator 2:	The next day was foggy and wet. Charlotte's web was truly a thing of beauty.
Narrator 3:	Lurvy discovered the first miracle. Written in the middle of the web were the words, "Some Pig." Lurvy ran to tell Mr. Zuckerman.
Lurvy:	I think you should come down to the pig pen right away, Mr. Zuckerman! Hurry!
Mr. Zuckerman:	Is something wrong with the pig?
Lurvy:	Well not exactly. Just come and see.
Mr. Zuckerman:	"Some Pig!" It's a miracle. Our pig is completely out of the ordinary! It's written in the spider's web!

Reader's Theater Script for Charlotte's Web *(cont.)*

Narrator 1:	Mrs. Zuckerman thought it was the spider who wasn't ordinary, but everyone who saw the web thought it was the pig who was special.
Charlotte:	See how easy it is to fool people? Now, what shall I write next?
Lurvy:	I think the next word we'll see in the web will be "Plump." That pig is really putting on weight.
Mr. Zuckerman:	I hope we'll see "Mr. Zuckerman's Pig" in the web. After all, it is MY pig.
Fern:	I hope Charlotte will write "Pretty" in her web. Wilbur is the prettiest pig I've ever seen.
Narrator 2:	(Speaking to the audience): Does anyone else have an idea for Charlotte—a word that does NOT appear in the book? Raise your hand if you have an idea? [Note: Narrator 2 can call on two or three people in the audience who have their hands up.]
Narrator 3:	Thank you for those ideas. I hope Charlotte was listening.
Old Sheep:	The goose has suggested "Terrific, Terrific, Terrific." What do you think, Charlotte?
Charlotte:	I like the word, "Terrific," but I think just one is enough.
Wilbur:	But, Charlotte, I'm NOT terrific. I'm just average for a pig.
Charlotte:	That doesn't make any difference. If people see the word "Terrific" in print, they will believe it. Humans are like that. Besides, you're terrific as far as I'm concerned, Wilbur.
Narrator 1:	The next morning, Wilbur stood under the web in which the word, "Terrific," appeared. Everyone was excited and came to see the famous pig.
Templeton:	What's going on here? What's all the excitement?
Old Sheep:	Just the rat we didn't want to see. But now that you're here, Templeton, maybe you can make yourself useful. Next time you go to the dump, bring back some clippings from a magazine, will you?
Charlotte:	I need new ideas to write in my web, Templeton. I'm trying to save Wilbur's life.
Templeton:	Why should I care about what happens to Wilbur?
Fern:	If Wilbur dies, his trough will be empty, and his leftovers are your chief source of food.
Templeton:	Hmmm. I guess you're right. Okay. I'll see what I can find at the dump.

Reader's Theater Script for Charlotte's Web *(cont.)*

Narrator 2: Templeton brought an advertisement from a magazine back from the dump. He carried it in his mouth.

Templeton: This ad says "Crunchy." Can you write that in your web?

Charlotte: Oh, no. "Crunchy" will make Zuckerman think of bacon. You'll have to go get another word, Templeton.

Templeton: I don't believe this! Do I look like a messenger boy? Why write about that silly pig, anyway? Write about ME, instead! You could write "Handsome" or "Smart" or "The Best Rat in the World."

Narrator 3: After some persuasion, Templeton made two more trips to the dump, and Charlotte finally had a new word... "Radiant."

Narrator 1: Everyone who came to see Wilbur when he was "Some Pig" and "Terrific" came back to see him looking "Radiant."

Narrator 2: Wilbur did his best to look radiant. He did all he could to make himself glow. He even did a flip with a back twist.

Narrator 3: Mr. Zuckerman decided to take his famous pig to the county fair. While they were at the fair, Charlotte wrote one more word in her web. The word was "Humble."

Narrator 1: Wilbur was awarded a special prize and fainted from all the excitement.

Narrator 2: Mr. Zuckerman was proud of Wilbur, and Wilbur knew his life would be spared.

Narrator 3: Wilbur was very grateful to Charlotte.

Wilbur: When I first met you, Charlotte, I thought you were blood-thirsty, but now you have saved my life. I don't deserve a friend like you.

Charlotte: You have been a good and loyal friend, Wilbur. That, in itself, is a tremendous thing.

Wilbur: You saved me, Charlotte, and I would gladly give my life for you.

Charlotte: I'm sure you would. Thank you, Wilbur.

Narrator 1: Charlotte and Wilbur were true friends to the very end.

Narrator 2: Wilbur had a chance to repay Charlotte when he carried her egg sac back to the farm.

Narrator 3: Wilbur never forgot what a wonderful friend Charlotte had been to him.

Announcer: Wilbur and Charlotte are now going to read a poem to each other. Listen for some of the descriptive words they use. *[Teacher: Two new children can be designated to read the poems on page 20. You may wish to involve small groups or assign half the class to read one poem, and the other half to read the second poem. Adapt the Announcer's preceding lines to fit the situation.]*

Announcer: We will now sing a song entitled "Some Pig!" *(When the song is finished the announcer or another student thanks the audience for coming and invites everyone to enjoy the food and classroom displays.)*

Bibliography

Back, Christine. *Spider's Web.* Silver, 1986.

Baker, Jeannie. *One Hungry Spider.* Dutton, 1983.

Bender, Lionel. *Spiders.* Gloucester, 1988.

Brooks, Walter R. *Freddy and the Perilous Adventure.* Knopf, 1986. (and other books in the *Freddy the Pig* series)

Brown, Margaret Wise. *Once Upon a Time in a Pigpen: And Three Other Stories.* HarperChild, 1980.

Browne, Anthony. *Piggybook.* Knopf, 1986.

Bryan,Ashley. *The Dancing Cranny.* Macmillan,1977.

Bushey, Jerry. *Farming the Land: Modern Farmers and Their Machines.* Carolrhoda, 1987.

Christelow, Eileen. *Mr. Murphy's Marvelous Invention.* Houghton Mifflin, 1983.

Climo, Shirley. *The Cobweb Christmas.* HarperChild, 1982.

Climo, Shirley. *Someone Saw a Spider: Spider Facts and Folktales.* HarperChild, 1985.

Gackenback, Dick. *The Pig Who Saw Everything.* Houghton Mifflin, 1978.

Geisert, Arthur. *Pa's Balloon and Other Pig Tales.* Houghton Mifflin, 1984.

Geisert, Arthur. *Pigs from A to Z.* Houghton Mifflin, 1986.

Goldin, Augusta. *Spider Silk.* HarperChild,1964.

Goodal, John S. *The Story of a Farm.* Macmillan, 1989.

Haley, Gail. *A Story, a Story.* Macmillan, 1970.

Hauptmann, Tatjana. *Day in the Life of Petronella Pig.* Smith, 1980.

Hawes, Judy. *My Daddy Longlegs.* HarperChild, 1972.

Heine, Helme. *The Pigs' Wedding.* Macmillan, 1986.

Heine, Helme. *Seven Wild Pigs: Eleven Picture Book Fantasies.* Macmillan, 1988.

Hoban, Lillian. *Mr. Pig and Sonny Too.* HarperChild, 1977.

Johnston, Tony. *Yonder.* Dial, 1988.

King-Smith, Dick. *Pigs Might Fly.* Viking, 1982.

Kraus, Robert. *How Spider Saved Halloween.* Dutton, 1980.

Krause, Ute. *Pig Surprise.* Dial,1989.

McDermott, Gerald. *Anansi, the Spider: A Tale from the Ashanti.* Holt, 1972.

McNulty, Faith. *The Lady and the Spider.* HarperChild, 1986.

Overbeck, Cynthia. *Curly the Piglet.* Carolrhoda, 1976.

Patent, Dorothy Hinshaw. *Spider Magic.* Holiday House, 1982.

Patterson, Geoffrey. *A Pig's Tale.* Andre Deutsch, 1983.

Pellowski, Anne. *Willow Wind Farm: Betsy's Story.* Putnam, 1981.

Rayner, Mary. *Garth Pig and the Ice Cream Lady.* Macmillan, 1977.

Rayner, Mary. *Mrs. Pig Gets Cross and Other Stories.* Dutton, 1987.

Rose, Anne. *Spider in the Sky.* HarperChild, 1978.

Saunders, Susan. *The Daring Rescue of Marlon the Swimming Pig.* Random House, 1987.

Scott, Jack Denton. *The Book of the Pig.* Putnam,1981.

Sharmat, Mitchell. *The Seven Sloppy Days of Phineas Pig.* Harcourt, 1983.

Slate, Joseph. *The Mean, Clean, Giant Canoe Machine.* HarperChild, 1983.

Stolz, Mary. *Emmett's Pig.* HarperChild, 1959.

Van Leeuwen, Jean. *More Tales of Amanda Pig.* Dial, 1985.

White, E.B. *Stuart Little.* HarperChild,1945.

White, E.B. *The Trumpet of the Swan.* HarperChild, 1970.

Williams, Garth. *Baby Farm Animals.* Western, 1983.

Yolen, Jane. *Picnic with Piggins.* Harcourt, 1988.